image of
Christ

C image of hrist

SAINT FRANCIS OF ASSISI

With a Foreword by
Alice von Hildebrand

Formerly published under the title
Not as the World Gives
St. Francis' Message to Laymen Today

Dietrich von Hildebrand

FRANCISCAN UNIVERSITY PRESS
Franciscan University of Steubenville
Steubenville, Ohio

Imprimi Potest: Dominic Limacher, OFM
Minister Provincial
Nihil Obstat: Mark Hegener, OFM
Censor Deputatus
Imprimatur: Most Rev. Cletus F. O'Donnell, DD
Vicar General
Archdiocese of Chicago

Published originally under the title *Not as the World Gives: St. Francis' Message to Laymen Today,* August 9, 1963, by Franciscan Herald Press, Chicago

1993 Publication by:
Franciscan University Press
Franciscan University of Steubenville
Steubenville, Ohio 43952

Cover Design: Dawn C. Harris

ISBN 0-940535-65-3

Contents

Foreword

This book, written on the occasion of the seven hundredth anniversary of the foundation of the Third Order of St. Francis, is a song of gratitude; indeed, the debt of my late husband to the Poverello, the little poor man of Assisi, was a great one, for God used this saint to reveal to him the beauty of the supernatural.

Born and raised in Florence, the son of loving parents and the last child of a family of six, Dietrich von Hildebrand had an exceptionally happy youth. Affection, beauty, the best of education, friendship: all of these great natural goods were given to him. But one thing was sadly lacking: religion. His parents were liberal Protestants, noble pagans really, and gave their only son no religious instruction. But God's grace touched him even as a child, when—alone in his whole family—he was granted belief in the divinity of Christ.

Convinced of the objectivity of truth, deeply touched by beauty in nature and art, he was to discover, through God's grace, that these natural goods are but faint reflections of the infinite beauty of God. This discovery took place when Max Scheler spoke to him about the phenomenon of sanctity which blossoms so frequently in the garden of the Catholic Church. To illustrate his thesis, Scheler sketched the personality of St. Francis, using his outstanding philosophical gifts to open to his friend the kingdom of the supernatural. For every saint is a mini-Tabor.

The sublimity of this realm is such that divine revelation alone can account for it. The word that it speaks clearly comes from heaven, the song that it sings unveils a transcendent reality for its harmonies are celestial. How inconceivable that a human creature unaided by grace would recognize the suffering Christ in a leper! How impossible for fallen man to love his enemies and pray for those who persecute him! How meaningless to give my cloak to someone who has already received my coat! And how absurd to experience "perfect joy" upon being badly treated, beaten, and refused access to a monastery in which, as a traveller, one hoped to find shelter!

And yet this spiritual revolution took place in Francis' life. This discovery touched Dietrich von Hildebrand to the very core of his being, and opened his eyes to a reality the existence of which he had not even suspected. A few years later, Blessed Edith Stein was to have the very same experience upon reading the life of St. Teresa of Avila, for the reality of sainthood is living proof that Christ's holy blood has redeemed the world. God chose both Francis and Teresa as his instruments to bring into the Church these two outstanding students of Edmund Husserl (both received their Ph.D.s under him), who thenceforth put their talents at the service of the holy Catholic Church, the Bride of Christ.

Francis of Assisi is probably the most popular yet least understood of all saints. Rare are those who understand the real Francis. So lovable is his personality that the temptation is great to love him for the wrong reasons and lose sight of his true message.

Francis is oft praised for his love of nature, and seen as a sort of pantheist; loved for his joyfulness and song, and seen as a cheerful troubadour. But what an abyss lies between a pantheistic conception of nature in which all things are parts of an immense whole called god, and Francis' relation to Brother the Sun, to Sister the Water which modestly sing God's praise. Close to him in their creaturehood, nevertheless both sun and water were far from him because they are only traces of God, whereas all human beings are God's images.

A clear understanding of Francis' personality and message requires a supernatural perspective. Francis was a saint, he was holy. Indeed, the real Francis' chief concern was to love God and to sing his praises as a herald and servant of Christ the King—no matter what the cost. Today's widespread misunderstanding of Francis exists precisely because the supernatural approach is sadly lacking. A case in point is the praise one writer recently showered on Mother Teresa for her efficiency and talent as an organizer, attempting to place her on a level with successful and "self-made" businessmen. Can one imagine a greater misunderstanding!

The song of this small book stands in stark contrast with such secular-minded evaluations. The author's supernatural perspective helps us see the true Francis, the Francis who wept because "Love was so little loved," the Francis who knew so well that "one thing alone is necessary."

Nevertheless, in Francis' life, the words of Christ "Seek ye first the kingdom of God and his justice, and the rest will be added unto you" find their fulfillment: for Francis was not a social reformer, yet Franciscan thought was the life-blood of amazing social reforms. Francis was not concerned about leaving his stamp on the arts, yet his spirit left a profound imprint on the literature, painting, sculpture, and architecture of the Trecento and Quattrocento—recall Giotto, Thomas of Celano, Jacoppone da Todi, Dante, and Franciscan architecture which so clearly reflect the Franciscan spirit.

Francis' only desire was to follow Christ, and Christ crucified. He lived in absolute poverty to imitate him who did not have a stone on which to lay his head. He put ashes on his food. He chose a rock as his pillow. He embraced the sufferings of the Holy Victim and became the image of Christ. Francis' asceticism teaches us detachment from earthly things, from the allurements of what is merely pleasurable.

The same Francis opens our eyes to the value and message of authentic human goods: beauty, truth, love, friendship—which reflect God and can lead us to him. Francis perfectly understood what my husband articulates herein, that while the human heart must detach itself from whatever is merely "subjectively satisfying," it is called upon to love all of God's creatures according to their rank, seeing them as messengers modestly singing the praise of the One in whom all things should be loved, and apart from whom none deserves to be loved at all.

It is proper and right that this book should be reprinted by a Franciscan university which aims at reviving the spirit of this great saint in contemporary American education.

ALICE VON HILDEBRAND

I

Seek First God's Kingdom

"Seek first the kingdom of God and his justice, and all these things will be given you besides" (Matt 6.33).

1

The Modern Man's Ailments

Every age reflects anew the great battle of the "Prince of this world" against the Savior of the world. In every age we see the waves of pride and concupiscence break against the kingdom of God on earth. We see apostasy, heresy, unbelief, hatred of God, impurity, indifference, and human respect rise against his kingdom. In a thousand ways, open and secret, these things seek to destroy the vineyard of the Lord, wherein the heroic spirit of sacrifice, strong faith, purity, self-denial, humility, and charity manifest themselves at all times. Every age, however, has its peculiar problems, and the enemy is always seeking new means and new ways to draw man's heart away from God. In our epoch the battle between Satan and Christ seems to reach a climax.

Humanity is at the crossroads. This is true whether we speak of the great debate between Communism and democracy, or of the entire spiritual situation.

The conflict between totalitarianism and democracy concerns the relation between the individual and the state. Totalitarianism claims an absolute sovereignty of the state over the individual and denies completely the rights of the person, who is conceived as nothing but a mere part of a collective entity; whereas democracy insists upon the inalienable rights of the individual and stresses the limits of state sovereignty according to natural law. This conflict, though a specifically drastic expression of the present crisis, is, however, but one aspect of the great decision at stake. In order to understand the entire impact of the crisis we have to dig deeper.

The real conflict is between Christianity on the one hand and a thoroughly anti-Christian conception of life on the other. This struggle has reached a decisive stage; it has become a radical clash between two worlds, embracing all domains of life and human existence. The liberal age was an age of compromise. Nothwithstanding its anticlericalism and its contention against Christian doctrine in the religious and philosophical fields, it retained Christian elements in the moral, sociological, juridical, and cultural spheres. Our present age, however, reveals a consistent, anti-Christian conception in every domain of life on the part of the enemies of Christianity.

The mark of the present crisis is man's attempt to free himself from his condition as a created being, to deny his metaphysical situation, to disengage himself from all bonds with anything greater than himself. Man endeavors to build a new Tower of Babel.

This self-sufficiency is characterized by the rejection of all bonds linking us to God and to moral law. The modern man who is affected by this perversion refuses to conform to the call of values, to surrender, to submit to something for its own sake, for the sake of its own intrinsic nobility and sublimity. Reverence, obedience, gratitude are alien to him. He does not want to abandon himself; on the contrary, everything becomes a means for his arbitrary pleasure and satisfaction. He looks upon marriage as something with which he can deal according to his arbitrary mood; not as a holy bond, something sublime that he is compelled to respect. He contracts marriages and gets divorces as he exchanges one glove for another. Instead of seeing in children a gift of God, he himself wants to determine their number by artificial birth control. On the one hand, he believes himself entitled to shorten the lives of others and his own by euthanasia, when they seem to him no longer worth while; on the other, he wishes to become forgetful of death, the tragic, implacable tribute of our creaturehood, as is evidenced in the cemeteries of Los Angeles which Evelyn Waugh stigmatizes in his work *The Loved One*.

Further—and here we touch an especially important point—he no longer wants to admit the existence of that factor in our life as creatures which is often called "chance" and which a Christian calls Providence. He himself wants to determine everything; he seeks to replace the rhythm of a truly human life with its constant dependence upon factors that we cannot ourselves control—the element of surprise, of a gift bestowed upon us, of bliss and trial—with a human insurance against all the unforeseen and unforeseeable elements. He wants to exclude by eugenics the possibility that men who are crippled or mentally deficient should have existence. He wants to exclude by human means the possibility of his having an unpleasant employer, of his depending upon the kindness and generosity of another person. He refuses to receive any gifts, but wants to claim everything as his right. He does not rejoice in experiencing the charity and generosity of his neighbors because these are factors which he has not himself determined and which call for gratitude.

He no longer approaches beauty in nature and art with reverence, as something reflecting a higher world above him. He treats beauty as something he relishes like a good wine. He makes no effort to seek beauty where it is, but wants it to be offered to him on a dish while he sits back and relaxes. He does not want to be raised above himself, to emerge from his own accustomed atmosphere; instead he wants beauty to be drawn into his realm as mere fun or entertainment.

He wants himself to be the source of all authority in community life. His is no longer the conception of democracy which determines the structure and the laws of community life according to the objective norms of right and wrong, and in which freedom consists in the fact that one is called to co-operate in finding what is objectively right. His concept of democracy means rather that the majority arbitrarily decides what is right and wrong, that the arbitrary will of the individual is the very source of right and wrong. In other words, the arbitrary will of the individual replaces the objective norm. Instead of believing that there is a chance that the majority of men will choose what is objectively right, what is right independently of their will, the modern man believes that their arbitrary decision makes a law right and legitimate.

The constantly growing secularization of life has reached a point today which leads to a corrosion and destruction even of nature in several fields. The denial of God, of our creaturehood, affects also the sense for natural morality, and has brought about a widespread rejection of any objective distinction between good and evil, between what is right and what is wrong.

We should not forget that apostasy does not carry forth a *status ante quo,* a situation of advent as it were, but that it perverts our natural relation to the universe even beyond the wounds inflicted by original sin. It is thus a great error to call the widespread amoral approach to life prevalent today a form of paganism. Imperfect as pagan morality may have been, the fundamental role of moral good and evil can also be found in a pagan world. Today, on the contrary, we witness an artificial stripping of the world of its moral substance, the looking at man and his life in a way which neutralizes it from a moral point of view. As soon as one artificially denies the tremendous reality of moral good and evil, one becomes blind towards the true nature of the human universe. With that denial, all depth, all tension, all real spiritual life is eliminated. This extends even to literature. If we artificially eliminate the categories of good and evil from *Othello*, the moral horror of a Iago, the tragic guilt of Othello, the purity and innocence of Desdemona, then, instead of this overwhelming tragedy, we have something without depth, without tension, without poetry. In seeing everyone as a product of complexes, and so on, you are transported into the office of a psychoanalyst which certainly—even for those who believe in this type of modern magician—does not convey any artistic beauty.

Certainly we can find single philosophers in former times, especially in antiquity, who deny the objective character of morality. But today the amorality also affects the existential approach to life of the average man.

This amoral attitude manifests itself especially in the sphere of sex. Not only the sense for the mystery of sex, for its meaning as a self-donation arising from a deep love, and implying the solemn will to form a sacred lasting bond has been lost; not only the feeling that sex is a garden into which we should enter only with the sanction of God has disappeared. No, even the natural basis of the relation of the two sexes, the tension, the thrill, the enrichment of human life which it represents, as well as all chivalrous feelings are disappearing more and more, and are being replaced by a dull comradeship. The reverence due the mystery of sex, and to persons of the other sex, as well as any sense of shame vanish more and more. Men no longer care whether the girl they marry is a virgin or whether she had numerous relationships. Even the elementary reaction of jealousy is waning.

The ominous element in this attitude is not only an increasing immorality but the amorality and its subsequent dehumanization of life, the destruction of elementary natural attitudes.

One believes that in neutralizing sex from the moral field one finally approaches it in a positive way. But in reality, the moral significance of this sphere is indissolubly linked with its true nature, with its true value, with the mystery it embodies. And in trying to draw sex out of the moral universe, one does not free the way for a "healthy" approach to sex, one does not make life happier, but one closes the door to the true approach towards sex, one makes man blind towards its true value; one bars the stream of deep happiness which it is destined to bestow on human life as a fulfillment of spousal love, in marriage. Instead of freeing man, one imprisons him in hopeless boredom.

It is not difficult to see the abyss which yawns between the conception of sexual intercourse as the satisfaction of a mere bodily instinct like hunger and thirst on the one hand, and the bodily union as the highest, mysterious fulfillment of spousal love, in the sacred bond of marriage, on the other. It is not difficult to see in which conception sex bears a higher value. But this cannot be grasped without seeing also that the abuse of something so deep and mysterious is a grave sin. We must realize that the attempt to exempt sex from the moral sphere, to deprive it of its moral significance, is really an enormous degradation of sex; we are not only pulling it down to a much lower level, but actually depriving it of all its true value. This is tantamount to dispossessing sex of its capacity to be a source of real happiness.

How the moral aspect is indissolubly linked to grasping the true nature of sex, becomes obvious as soon as we compare the following two cases: in the one an isolated sexual desire or a superficial intoxication which assumes the character of an overwhelming passion brings someone to fall. He is clearly aware of the moral evil which he is committing. He sees the mystery of the sexual sphere, its depth, its intimacy, its impact. He succumbs to the other aspect which this sphere can have, the mysterious, diabolic attraction.

In this case, there is also the terrible desecration; but at least he still sees the mystery of this sphere, because he is aware of the desecration, and because he grasps the moral abyss into which he is falling.

On the other hand, that man who sees sex as morally neutral, and sexual intercourse as a normal satisfaction of a healthy instinct like taking food, completely misses the true nature of sex. He is blind towards its intimacy, depth, impact, towards its mystery. He is still more unable to understand the role of the bodily union as fulfillment of a deep spousal love, he is still more cut off from the deep happiness which sex is destined to bestow on man, than the first man was.

Amorality is worse than immorality. The immoral man can repent his moral failure, he can turn back to his depth, whereas the amoral man has condemned himself to the periphery and finds no way back, when he has committed something objectively immoral.

The one who sins, but is aware of his immorality, still remains in the orbit of truth; he acknowledges the ultimate importance of the moral question, even if he goes astray at the moment. He still moves in the great true spiritual universe, and sees the true values. His situation may be tragic. However, the one who desecrates the mystery of sex by seeing in it a harmless satisfaction of a bodily instinct, the one who approaches the world trying to extinguish the light of morality, moves in a dull, falsified world, a world without depth, without thrill, without grandeur. He is not tragic, but he is immersed in hopeless boredom.

Hand in hand with this ostracizing of the categories of good and evil goes a widespread general prejudice, namely the belief that the only valid, authentic reality is the one which natural science presents to us. The rest is considered "romance." Many believe that it is in the laboratory alone that we touch valid, authentic reality.

This laboratory view grants reality only to things which are accessible to natural science. It replaces the human, existential aspect of the universe, the one which is presented to us in experience, by the one which natural science offers to us. It makes all values, all spiritual entities, all that which really forms our human life, which is the source of our happiness, a mere lovely illusion, a "romance."

Reverence is the mother of all virtues; but amorality goes hand in hand with the absolute decline of reverence. And linked with irreverence is the ideal of "taking it easy," of letting ourselves go, of believing that in doing so we manifest our freedom, we testify to our healthy spontaneity.

The tendency to let ourselves go, is deeply rooted in human nature. But in former times, even in antiquity, and especially in the Christian world, we were aware of the need to fight this tendency. The Christian understood that our demeanor should be an expression of our inner *sursum corda,* of the awareness of our bond to God, the *religio.* One aimed at a noble demeanor and saw it in no way as something artificial, but as an adequate expression of the inner attitude towards which we, at least, aim. The fact that one's exterior life was subject to certain forms, was in no way considered a denial of true spontaneity.

But today, and this is especially true for this country, the absence of form is considered a virtue. The inner attitude which expresses itself in this lack of form, the letting ourselves go, the enjoyment in letting ourselves be drawn downward, has become an idol. This pseudo-naturality has become the object of a cult.

God grants to the apostate a time of respite concerning the repercussions of his apostasy in the field of culture, of his relation to natural goods. In looking at history, we can see how certain epochs, notwithstanding a recess in the domain of faith, still bring forth beautiful flowers in the cultural field. The cultural and human inspiration which is originally a result of the Christian faith, is still alive though its source—faith—is vanishing. But after a certain time, the disease subsequent to apostasy also pervades all human realms. Today, we are witnessing the fact that the terrible sin of apostasy manifests itself not only in the religious realm, not only in an immoral life, but in all natural dimensions of human life; that the very basis of nature is corroded and perverted. The consequence of this dehumanization of life is a terrible "boredom," a boredom which leads inevitably to despair. In no other epoch were there so many suicides, so many cases of mental disease. Does not all this decomposition and desubstanzialization of human life convey to us the call of God: *"Jerusalem, Jerusalem, convertere ad Dominum Deum tuum"?* Do these consequences of the apostasy from Christ not invite us to an unconditioned following of Christ? Should they not awaken us to a new and deeper religious life, to a total surrender to Christ?

Great is the responsibility of all those who received the unmerited grace to be members of the Mystical Body of Christ. We should ask ourselves: How far is our infidelity, lukewarmness, mediocrity responsible for all these distortions? Have we really irradiated Christ, have we conveyed his message to the world, or have we failed in the apostolate of being?

In how far have we fulfilled the mission to which St. Peter exhorts us: "That you may declare his virtues who has called you out of darkness into his admirable light?"

The saints have fulfilled this mission, though they were human creatures as we are, with all the frailty of human nature and the wounds of original sin. They were able to put on *("induere")* Christ, to be transformed by Christ, to irradiate him. And there is perhaps no other saint in whom this transformation in Christ is so visible, so palpable as in St. Francis of Assisi, who was called an *alter Christus,* another Christ.

We propose to immerse ourselves in the contemplation of this saint, and listen to the appeal for our conversion which it conveys to us. For many, his personality and the Franciscan type of piety will be the way to a closer union with Christ, the way of sanctification. And the Third Order, such as it was intended by St. Francis, will be for many the way leading to a full surrender to Christ, and contribute to the overcoming of the specific dangers of our present epoch in Christ and with Christ.

2

The Spirit of Saint Francis

In every saint there is repeated in some way the wonder of Mt. Tabor, when God, for a brief moment, lifts the veil that conceals his kingdom of supernatural, mysterious glory and holiness from fallen men, when he allows one of the true followers of Christ to blossom among us. Perhaps in no other of the multitude who stand "in white garments before the throne of the Lamb" is this fact is more strikingly borne out than in St. Francis of Assisi. When we contemplate his life, from the time of his conversion until his death, a world of grace and of supernatural glory is disclosed to us. The life of a man, who is "flesh of our flesh" and "blood of our blood," who possesses not only the infirmities of creatures "except sin" but also this weakness, and feels in his body "the law of Adam," but who found his strength in the grace of the Most High Lord and was totally immersed in Jesus, "the splendor of eternal light," and was permeated with "the fragrance of Jesus" and reflected the brightness of "the Sun of justice." Holiness is not merely moral perfection or great natural goodness; it is the epitome and the crown of supernatural virtue, a mysterious reflection of the thrice holy, eternal Lord; it is the "light from Light," a radiation from God, which cannot be explained but only venerated with loving and reverent imitation, with head bowed and hands folded, as we begin to see what the saints see with such clarity and undimmed brilliance.

The modern, unbelieving world has taken to no other saint or treated him with such great sympathy as it has done with St. Francis. Yet at the same time no other saint is so misunderstood or misinterpreted as is St. Francis. Some have made him a pantheist; others a lovely troubadour, a romantic worshipper of nature; others again have seen in him a subjectivist and a forerunner of Luther. All these interpretations are false; they come from the spirit of the world. Only he who sees Francis as the most faithful son of the holy, infallible Church, "the mother of saints"; only he who views Francis' life as a true imitation of Christ, "the crown of all the saints"; only he who acknowledges every detail of Francis' life as the effect of the all-conquering, all-redeeming love of Jesus;—only he can comprehend the nature of this most radiant of all saints. Whoever contemplates objectively this saintly figure, of whom it can be truthfully said, "he lives, now not he, but Christ lives in him," must feel how wrong is all such talk of him as a "life's artist," or "a modern saint," and how far from the truth are all these terms, expressive of the spirit of the times, with regard to one who is encircled with the bright light of eter-

28

nity. He set up no program, neither for social reforms nor for anything else. He was no "sage" who claimed to have found the secrets of peace of soul and contentment. He was a saint, one of those "remarkable servants of God who appear from time to time in the Catholic Church as angels in human form and diffuse their light as they go their way to heaven" (Newman, *Discourses to Mixed Congregations*).

In the life of the saints everything is inspired by the fact that there is an "almighty, all-knowing, all-merciful God, who is absolute Lord"; that Jesus, the God-man lives; that to redeem mankind he did not "shun the Virgin's womb"; that he overcame "the sting of death" and opened heaven for the faithful, "the heavenly Jerusalem," "Mt. Sion," where Jesus, "the Sun of justice," reigns, which is inhabited by the angels and archangels, where the Blessed Virgin, immaculately conceived, looks graciously upon us, the Mother of God and our mother, who is called by the Church "the gate of heaven," where all the saints stand before the face of God and praise and glorify him in eternal adoration and love. Picture Francis, praying at night in tears and repeating over and over again, *"Deus meus et omnia,"* "My God and my all." "Pure hearts disdain earthly things and seek the heavenly; they look to the Lord, the living and true God, with pure heart and soul, and continuously adore him." Thus Francis exhorted his disciples. Francis, who passed his days and nights in the most intimate union with God, who traversed the world as the "herald of the great King," inebriated with love for Jesus.

With a life centered in Jesus and radiating from him in whose heart beats "the fulness of the Godhead," a deep awareness of sin, and a spirit of genuine penance are inseparably present. A saint who looks ever to God, is on fire with the love of Jesus, is overcome with the sweetness of Jesus, necessarily also shudders at the sight of sin, also has deep contrition for his own sins, and is pierced through and through with sorrow over the sinfulness of the world and the thousand offenses committed daily against God. "Weep over yourselves and over your sins." The saint alone sees and understands the true condition of man; he alone is filled with a consciousness of the "one thing necessary"; he sees everything focused in the eternal light, *in conspectu Dei*. This contrition and this clarity of vision concerning one's own condition are the source of that longing for penance that burned in St. Francis, who covered his food with ashes and slept on a rock on La Verna's heights; who treated his body so severely that at the end of his life he expressed sympathy for Brother Ass, as he called his body.

This life in Jesus and with Jesus, which is characteristic of the saints, whose "conversation is in heaven," presupposes humility, a blissful surrender to God, the Creator of heaven and earth, the surrender of one who not only thinks little of himself but does not want to be more than the most submissive servant of the Lord, who blissfully rests in God, in unconditional obedience, in adoring submission, freed from all self-centeredness.

Where do we find this victory over self, this blotting out of every remnant of pride and self-importance, this blissful, victorious freedom but in him who struck "the world" a blow in the face as he walked the streets of his native city, a beggar in tattered clothing, yet recognized as the son of a rich merchant; who, to humiliate himself, made public his alleged faults; who let himself be dragged, half naked, with a halter around his neck, along the stony floor of the church, where he confessed his faults so that the people might recognize him as a glutton; who ordered a brother to call him a fool, a stupid, useless knave, and then said: "May the Lord bless you, my beloved son, for you speak the truth; such words must the son of Peter Bernardone listen to"; who fed himself on the refuse he had received by begging; who welcomed being a fool for Christ's sake and gave his order the name of "Friars Minor," or Lesser Brethren. Listen to the words of St. Francis himself:

"I do not take myself for a Lesser Brother unless I shall be of the disposition I will describe to you. Suppose that as the superior of the brothers I go to the chapter, preach to the brothers, remonstrate with them, and at last they speak up against me: 'We have no use for an unlettered, inferior man, so we do not want you ruling over us, without all art of expression and plain and unpolished as you are.' Finally, I am thrown out in disgrace, despised by them all. I tell you, unless I listen to that talk with the same brow, the same cheer of mind, and the same determination of holiness, I am by no means a Lesser Brother."

"If humility is the highest of the human virtues, then love is a divine virtue." Love is the very life of the saints, and it permeates and transfigures all of their manifestations. It is not merely natural love, neither is it mere obedience to God's law, nor good will toward one's neighbor. But it is the supernatural love of God and of neighbor that is greater, more intense than all natural love; for supernatural love is the bright, crystal-clear stream that is free from all murky passion; it is the free, victorious love of which St. Paul says: "Charity is never perverse or proud; has no selfish aims, does not brood over injury, takes no pleasure

31

in wrongdoing, sustains, believes, hopes, endures to the last."

Does not this blessed spirit of love overpower us as we approach the truest of all the followers of Christ, who was "inebriated with Christ"; who, at the crib of Greccio, licked his lips covered with sweetness as often as he spoke the name of Jesus; who tenderly picked up the worms along the road lest they be trampled upon, because he remembered these words of the Master, "I am a worm and no man"; who burned within at the words, "the love of God"; who longed for nothing more ardently than a martyr's death for Jesus? "I beseech you, O Lord, that the fiery and honey-sweetened strength of your love may free my soul from all that is under heaven, that I may die out of love for you, who deigned to die out of love for me." Does not our heart expand when we see Francis kissing the festering sores of the leper, from whom he at first shrank with a violent revulsion? Are we not moved by his tender show of love to Brother Leo, whom he called "the lamb of God," when Brother Leo was deeply troubled because he thought Francis did not love him as much as formerly, and by the words of the holy blessing he wrote for Leo on a scrap of paper to heal his heartaches: "The Lord bless you and keep you. May he show his face to you and have mercy on you. May he turn his countenance to you and give you peace. The Lord bless you, Brother Leo."

Whose heart is not pierced by the victorious ray of supernatural love when he sees Francis cross the sea alone to visit the sultan and to bring the light of faith to the Saracens; Francis, who once said, "nothing may be preferred to the saving of souls"; Francis, who bore the sufferings of the sick and ate meat on a fast day—Francis, the man of penance—so that the sick would not feel embarrassed in eating; Francis, who publicly begged meat for them on a fast day, who loved his own so much that he believed he would not attain salvation if he did not lead to glory those who were entrusted to him; Francis, who brought to shame all natural notions of measure and prudence, and all natural ways of living by his foolishness of the cross; Francis, who was inebriated with the love of Jesus, "the sweet rapture of saints," "the joy of angels," whose heart the Church calls the "burning furnace of charity." When one sees this love permeate the whole person of St. Francis, when one sees him considering himself in the deepest humility to be the greatest of sinners—he who in the presence of God is overcome with the glory and sweetness of the Lord and is transfigured—one must bow his head in reverence and say with thankfulness to God: "May the saints praise you, O Lord; may they make known the glories of your kingdom!"

The saints reflect all the supernatural virtues and gifts of the Holy Spirit; for, the gifts of the Holy Spirit cannot be separated. Yet every saint exemplifies a unique form and expression of holiness. There is something common to all, namely, a life lived in and through and for Jesus, though this life bears fruit in each saint in a special way. In St. Francis we find a love that is full of sweet regard for all creation, even for non-living things.

"He called all creatures brothers and with secret art penetrated to the inner nature of every creature with the sharp look of his heart, as if he had entered already into the freedom of the glory of the children of God." These words of Thomas of Celano describe the love with which St. Francis embraced all creatures, for he saw in them the creatures of "the all-good, the all-holy Lord, Creator of heaven and

33

earth." He saw them all in relation to Jesus, whose heart the Church terms "the desire of the everlasting hills." This love of St. Francis, which set out honey and wine for the bees so that they would not suffer unduly during the cold days of winter, found in the flowers of the field an incentive to praise God and saw the "cornfields and the vineyards, the beauty of the meadows, every ripple of the stream, the green of gardens, the earth, fire, wind—all these as praising God." His heart was flooded with inexpressible joy as he beheld the sun, the moon, and the stars. And all of this was the very opposite of the attitude of a pantheist. St. Francis loved all these things, not as if he felt himself in a living oneness with "Mother Nature"; but he loved them all because he saw all creatures as coming from the heavenly Father, "whose wonders the heavens praise." He felt himself close to each individual existing thing, and he called them all brother and sister and praised God "for Brother Sun, which ushers in the day and shines down upon us bright and brilliant, and is a reflection of the Most High." He invited the sun to praise God with him. He took care not to spill water where it would be trampled upon, because water was for him a symbol of the sacrament of penance and was holy because water was used in baptism. He picked up every scrap of paper that had writing on it, because the letters could form the Most Holy Name of Jesus, at whose name "everything in heaven and on earth and under the earth must bend the knee" (Phil. 2-10). Or picture St. Francis approaching a farmer carrying two little lambs to the market to be slaughtered. Francis was moved with pity and gave the farmer the mantle he had just received from a rich man for the lambs and then set them free; for, he loved lambs, which reminded him of the words

34

of John the Baptist, who said of Jesus, "Behold, the lamb of God, who takes away the sin of the world" (Jn. 1, 29).

This was no pantheist idolization of nature, nor the harmless natural love of animals, typical of so many good-hearted people today; this was an outpouring of his ravishing love for Jesus, the kind of love for Jesus that liberates the soul and opens the eyes; a love that sees all things, even the natural, in a supernatural light; a love that reveals the mysterious and wonderful workings of God's love in creation and the splendor which everything good and beautiful acquires through the Word becoming Flesh. "In the beautiful he saw the Most Beautiful; and in the traces impressed by God on things, he sought him whom his soul loved. Christ Jesus, the Crucified, was ever before his mind's eye, and he wished in his burning love to be wholly transformed into him."

But he who loved natural creation with a supernatural love, loved first of all the kingdom of God on earth, the Church, born of the Blood of Christ, the Bride of Christ; and above all he loved the most Blessed Sacrament, over which arched the whole Church like an immense tabernacle.

"I beseech you, therefore, my brethren, as I kiss your feet, with all the love I am capable of, that you show all possible reverence and honor to the most holy Body and Blood of our Lord Jesus Christ, through whom all that is in heaven and on earth is reconciled to God."

What love and respect he had for priests, who had power over the Body of the Lord. He admonished his brethren to consider them as masters in what concerns the salvation of souls and does not contradict the order's rule. Francis often said: "If I were to meet at the same time a saint from

35

heaven and a poor priest, I would first show my respect to the priest and quickly kiss his hand, and then I would say: 'O wait, St. Lawrence, for the hands of this man touch the Word of Life and possess a good that spreads far over mankind.' "

Love of the cross filled his soul, but also love of the newborn Christ, on whose feast "even the walls should have meat." What inexpressible love, too, he felt for the all holy Virgin and Mother of God, because she gave us as Brother the eternal King of glory. Francis addressed her in these words: "Hail, holy Lady! Most holy Queen! Mary, Mother of God, yet a virgin forever! Hail, his handmaiden! Hail, his Mother!" Under her protection he placed his whole order, for, after Christ, he placed his greatest confidence in her. Recall also the love he had for St. Michael, for the Apostles Peter and Paul, whose tombs he visited at the very outset of his conversion. Recall his reverence for holy relics, for the pope, the Vicar of Christ, to whom he pledged obedience. Yes, that victorious, overflowing, and ardent love for Jesus, the crucified God-man—a love of which St. Paul said, "Charity never fails" (1 Cor. 13, 8)— was the fulcrum of his life; and it embraced all, for he recognized in all the face of Jesus. But above all there was in him a glowing love for what came through Jesus, the kingdom of God on earth.

Whoever becomes interested in St. Francis will find him surrounded by an aureole of heavenly joy in a rather unique way. His was not the gay and cheerful temperament that bubbles over without restrain; his was not the exuberant joy of living that still is unable to weather sudden storms. His was a crystal-clear and soaring holy joy that was filled with the peace of Jesus Christ, a joy akin to that

36

of the angels and saints in heaven; the kind of joy that lights up only at the existence of God, who is the "most high, most good, most mighty, most almighty; most merciful and most just; most hidden and most present; most beautiful and most strong; stable and incomprehensible; unchangeable and yet changing all things; never new and never old, yet renewing all things" (Conf. I, 4). It is the joy kindled by Jesus, whose heart is "the delight of all the saints," who is "the most beautiful of the children of men," and who says of himself: "I am the way, the truth, and the life." His was that supernatural, blessed joy, which even the noblest gifts of this life, taken by themselves, cannot bestow upon us the joy unkindled through Jesus Christ, "through whom a new light of glory shines in the eyes of our spirit"; the joy enkindled by the smile of the most Blessed Virgin Mary; the joy that comes from the choirs of angels, from "the white, gleaming host of martyrs," from all creation, natural and supernatural, even from the smell of the flowers and the rushing of the waters of a stream when seen in Christ. Who would not rejoice in the presence of this graudeur, "rejoicing in the Lord!" Yes, this joy brightens up before us as we read of St. Francis that, having given up all earthly things, he was inebriated with love of Jesus. Wandering one day through the countryside of Assisi, he was stopped by robbers who asked him who he was. In a rapture of joy, Francis exclaimed, "I am the herald of the great king." The robbers answered by throwing him into a ditch filled with snow and calling out as they went their way, "Lie there, foolish herald of God!" Francis got up and from a heart filled with joy sang a song of praise that echoed through the woods around Assisi. Who does not recognize the supernatural in this joy of Francis, a joy full of the peace that "the world cannot give."

Again picture St. Francis with Brother Masseo as they feast at a spring in highest poverty on pieces of bread begged along the way, with a stone as a table, and Francis crying out loudly, "O Brother Masseo, we are not worthy of such a treasure." He was filled with gratitude toward God who had prepared for them, without any contribution on their part, such a "kingly meal"—with a stone so wide and smooth; with water so pure and clear for drinking; with bread so strengthening. Not that he enjoyed the food so much and therefore gave thanks to God; but these gifts of nature are experienced by him as irradiations of divine goodness; they were a mouthpiece of God's divine love, a window of his supernatural glory. Yes, a holy, supernatural joy thrilled his whole being and tuned his whole life to a song of praise of God's eternal glory, goodness, and love.

The sweetest response of his joyous spirit often found expression in a song in French; and the divine whisperings that stole into his heart often burst forth in songs of jubilation in that language. At times he took a stick of wood, placed in on his left arm, and holding in his right hand a twig, bent by a string, he pretended to be playing on a violin, all the while singing lustily in French.

"Francis, poor and humble, enters heaven clothed in riches." All the saints were poor in their manner of living, free of all earthly possessions, free at least in spirit. St. Francis was the poorest of the saints and the most ardent lover of poverty. "Know, Brethren, that poverty is the special way of salvation; it is the nourishment of humility, the root of perfection, the treasure hidden in the field, as mentioned in the Gospel. To gain it one must sell all one has, but the sacrifice made is as nothing when compared to what is gained." These words Francis spoke when the brothers asked him at one of the chapters what virtue was most pleasing to the Lord. Think of Francis, how he bypassed Bologna when he heard that a house had been built there for the brothers and was known as the "house belonging to the brothers." He gave orders that the house should be abandoned at once. Think of Francis, how he rebuked a brother who had touched money. "Money and dung are of the same value," he remarked. He thought he should be even poorer than he was; and when a poor man who had absolutely nothing met him along the way, he said emphatically: "This poor man puts us to shame, for we have chosen poverty to gain riches, but poverty shines more resplendently in this man."

It was not just a wise prudence of the man who does not wish to get over-attached to earthly goods because such attachment could deprive him of his inner peace, nor the love of an austere life that was the source of his love of poverty; but it was the strong desire to be like his divine Master, to belong entirely to him who once said: "You cannot serve both God and Mammon," and "The foxes have dens, and the birds of the air have nests; but the Son of man has nowhere to lay his head" (Mt. 6,24; 8,20). The love of St. Francis did not restrict itself to poverty concerning external possessions, but also included being independent of the non-material goods of this world, like respect, honors, reputation, knowledge, science, and scholarship, according to the words of our Savior: "Blessed are the poor in spirit, for theirs is the kingdom of heaven" (Mt. 5,3).

"Whoever would reach these heights must renounce not only worldly prudence and wisdom, but also science, and completely detached, abandon himself into the arms of the crucified Savior; he does not renounce the world completely who in his innermost heart keeps a shrine lighted for his own ego." These are the words of St. Francis.

It was not a distrust of learning in favor of sound common sense, nor a mistrust of learning out of sympathy for the simplicity of the ordinary people, that was the motive of Francis' love of poverty in spirit. Francis made a voluntary renunciation of all human learning, scientific and popular, because such a renunciation makes one like a beggar ready to receive with open arms the incomparable wisdom of Jesus Christ.

Who does not think of these words of Jesus, "I praise you, Father, Lord of heaven and earth, that you hid these things from the wise and prudent, and revealed them to little ones" (Mt. 11, 25), as he contemplates the holy simplicity of the poorest of the poor, who wanted no studies for his order, who showed a special affection for his Brother John, because in his simplicity John imitated every movement of Francis? Francis did not oppose science as such, and above all not the sacred theology of the Doctors of the Church, but he did oppose reliance on one's own natural gifts and natural learning, for he insisted on these words of the Master, "If anyone wishes to come after me, let him deny himself," and on the spirit of humility and complete detachment that are necessary for the reception of the heavenly wisdom of the Holy Spirit, in the presence of which all natural knowledge and all natural greatness are but foolishness and empty talk. Whoever fixes his gaze on this figure surrounded by light, in whom "the grace of God has not been vain" will find "the heavens opening up before his eyes like a supernatural light that flashes like lightning through the dark clouds of the night."

Who does not see that last full measure of the freedom of "the children of God" encompassing Francis who surrendered his soul to Christ, who was "hidden with Christ in God," who crushed pride and concupiscence to win the love of Jesus?

Think of Francis as a youth, standing disrobed before the bishop, giving everything back to his father, even his garments and shirt; hear him cry out with joy, "Now I can truly say: "Our Father who art in heaven." Think of his ideal of perfect joy: when one is tired out and drenched with rain and hungry, and comes to a friary and is refused admission by the porter; when one keeps on knocking and is answered with blows, and then goes away, dirty and cold, to spend the night somewhere else; when one feels free of everything, even of one's own self, and finds rest in God and in total surrender to him,—that is perfect joy. This is the final freedom of one who seeks first the kingdom of God and finds that then all else is given to him too.

The words of the Gospel, "Take nothing for your journey, neither staff, nor wallet, nor bread, nor money (Lk. 9,3), gave Francis the basic rule of the life he chose for himself and his brethren, the life of following Jesus literally in a blissful surrender to Divine Providence, a life in which "all care is cast upon the Lord, and in which one has put on Christ and the crucified One." Do we not breathe the air of blessed freedom that comes to us from these words of Jesus: "Consider how the lilies of the field grow; they neither toil nor spin; and yet I say to you that not even Solomon in all his glory was arranged like one of these (Mt. 6,28), when we see Francis, surrounded by his first disciples, walking through the world, a pilgrim in supernatural

41

security and freedom? In them, we witness the conscious-ness of being pilgrims, the detachment which enables them to traverse the world as pilgrims, because they recognize with supernatural clarity what goods alone are compatible with the imitation of Christ. It is the soaring rhythm of life in those who, though they are in the world, are not of the world, which compels them to go from place to place and settle down in no one place because they know that their "abode is in heaven."

Yes, his abode was in heaven, he who like St. Stephen, the first martyr, saw the heavens open; he who was trans-formed in such an extraordinary way by the love of Jesus, that he was deigned to bear the stigmata of our Lord in his body; he whose heart was enraptured with the sweetness of Jesus so that he became the fool of him whose Sacred Heart is our "peace and reconciliation," a fool filled with the foolishness of the cross; he who struck the world a blow in the face; he, the humble, simple man of humility, the truest, most obedient son of the Holy Church, who, in supernat-ural joy and in deepest sorrow of heart and in the spirit of penance, walked through the world, casting rays of light all about him, even up to the hour when, singing, he ac-cepted death, when he could make his own the words of Jesus, "the Sun of justice," "well done, good and faithful servant; enter into the joy of the master" (Mt. 25, 23).

Not only is the wonder of Mt. Tabor repeated in every saint, when, for a brief moment, the heavens open; but, in a certain sense, every saint re-enacts the most sublime of all wonders, "the eternal Word's becoming flesh." For every saint whose life is in Christ, is a new realization of God's kingdom on earth, a new creation of the Holy Spirit, who overshadows the most blessed Virgin, and whom Jesus called the Comforter. The saint is not only a mirror in which we see the glory of God; but he is also a vessel of honor, an incarnation of a ray of God's glory, by which the world is enlightened, and the flame of love for the crucified Christ grows brighter. We see then, as the brilliance of this figure sheds its luster round about, and took roots in his disciples; we understand how the face of the earth was renewed by his true followers in his three orders. "As the morning star shines amid the clouds and as the moon reflects the brilliance of the sun, so does he shine in the temple of God. Alleluja, Alleluja."

3

The Influence of Saint Francis

We are told that Pope Innocent III once had a vision in a dream that the basilica of the Lateran in Rome *"omnium urbis et orbis ecclesiarum mater et caput"* had started to shake and was threatening to collapse. At that moment, a small poor man in the garments of a beggar suddenly appeared and by supporting the immense building upon his weak shoulders saved it from complete ruin. Later, when Francis Bernardone came to ask the Pope for approval of his and his followers' way of life, the Holy Father recognized him as the poor beggar he had seen in his vision.

This dream illustrates the exceptional influence that the life of St. Francis had upon the world. St. Francis, the son of a rich merchant of Assisi in Italy, was born at a time when there were great religious disturbances in the Christian world; a time of secularization, of bloody wars, of political and social tensions. He renounced all that procures honor and power, as well as wealth and respect in his own town, and chose instead to follow a beggar's way of life. By doing this he exerted a greater influence on his time than anyone else.

A youth, highly gifted and of fiery spirit, loving the splendor of the world, generous, brave, cheerful, munificent, chivalrous, the pride of his rich and well-respected father, and always a leader among his friends, suddenly decides to change his whole life by renouncing all the worldly goods that are his by birth. He frees himself from these material chains and chooses the life of the lowest beggar, and, as a result, becomes a target for the mockery of the boys on the street and a scandal to his father. But he has only one wish, namely, to lead a life exactly like that of the apostles according to the ways and teachings of the Gospel; and this youth gained an influence far greater than any prominent man of his days.

Francis founded two great religious orders: the First Order for men, the Order of Friars Minor; the Second Order for women, the Poor Clares; from both these orders an immense crowd of saints has issued. Through the centuries, and on up to and including our own day, members of these two orders have lived and are living a life for Christ and with Christ; and by so doing, they have been and continue to be a constant reminder to mankind of the "one thing that is necessary."

Yet Francis also founded an order for laymen, the Third Order, in which those who remain in the "world" and continue to practice their profession, renounce the spirit of the world, in order to live a new life in Christ and for Christ.

And with this Third Order, to which **Dante**, **Michelangelo**, **Columbus** later belonged, a completely new spirit entered into the Italian society of the Thirteenth Century, rifted by wars and social contrasts. Fighting parties were reconciled; cities at war with one another made peace; the poor looked upon their poverty in a new light; the rich opened up their hearts to the distress and need of the poor and the sick, especially the lepers, who in earlier times had been avoided like outcasts, and who, from that time on, received loving care. The spirit of unlimited avarice and unrestrained desire for enjoyment gave way to a recollection of the one thing necessary and a newly awakened love for Christ the Crucified; and this new love led to a new devotion to Christ's Mystical Body, the Church, and to a spirit of humble obedience to the Vicar of Christ on earth, the pope. A spirit of peace and love, a spirit free from pride and concupiscence spread everywhere and changed the features of Italian society of that time. Also in the world of creative spirit, particularly in the world of art, a new spring blossomed. The personality of this man, who in the most radical way renounced all the material goods of this life, had an unbelievably fruitful influence on the development of poetry and the fine arts. From him, for instance, came the deepest inspiration for classical Italian poetry; and by his influence upon the arts, he became the spiritual father of the Trecento and early Quattrocento, an epoch of immense fruitfulness in Italy.

Indeed, the dream-vision of Pope Innocent was fulfilled in Francis. Countless multitudes of people were converted and aroused to a new life in Christ by the light that this unique personality emanated. Once again the spirit of holy ardor and religious fervor, the life of faith and love, animated the members of the Mystical Body. The Church officially venerates as saints and blessed, more than three hundred and fifty sons and daughters of St. Francis. But, as we saw, this new life also spread far beyond the boundaries of the purely religious sphere. It had its influence on all areas of human life. The influence of St. Francis on art and poetry, although unplanned, is especially striking because it is greater than the influence of any other saint.

Various elements in the Franciscan spirit account for its inspirational influence on art and poetry. First of all, the Franciscan relationship with nature: instead of the prevalent symbolic conception of the exterior world, with the still characteristic reserve of the Middle Ages towards all direct, intuitive approaches to nature, Franciscanism emphasized a loving interest in every individual creature; a specifically intuitive, direct approach to nature. Whereas, before Francis, one had eschewed listening to the specific message given by visible and audible things, and sought the way leading to God primarily in the conceptual meaning of existing things and of creation, St. Francis viewed the appearance of the world offered to our senses, as a specific expression of the glory and bounty of God. It goes without saying that this Franciscan relationship to nature, seeing in nature a reflection of God's infinite beauty, could never give birth to naturalism in art.

Yet, the spring in art and poetry which was brought about by St. Francis was not only due to a new relation to nature. It was also due to the mysterious intrinsic poetry and charm of the very personality of St. Francis, a charm which emanated from every word spoken by him, from every expression. The personality of every saint has a sublime beauty: the very beauty of holiness. And in every saint this beauty has a specific individual note. But in St. Francis, this individual note finds a matchless and adequate expression. He expresses every idea and every experience in a totally unconventional, direct, and intensely personal manner. There is a poetic charm and beauty in his personality which is absolutely unique; the combination of a touching innocence with a natural innate simplicity such as we find only in a lovely child, and a holy wisdom, an ultimate seriousness and depth, a sweetness and meekness interwoven with a holy folly. Perhaps, St. Francis is the saint in whom the unique beauty of humility takes its most outspoken palpable form, materializes in a unique way all manifestations of his personality. Perhaps, he is also the saint who possesses the greatest originality.

The first fruit of this multifold fecundation of art through the spirit of St. Francis, is to be found in the great moving hymn called *The Canticle of the Sun,* which contains a whole world of lyrical beauty. It is the first poem in the Italian language. But other writings of Francis also exhale a poetic atmosphere on the highest level. This artistic spring is also visible in various, more or less, contemporary biographies of St. Francis, especially the *Fioretti,* a matchless work of art, in which an immediate naiveté, a poetic charm, and an inspired greatness are organically interwoven.

Art in the Thirteenth Century is imbued with a spring-like radiance. To the sublime greatness of the culture of the early Middle Ages, to the strength of Byzantine painting and Romantic plastic art, was added a touch of bright loveliness and tender sweetness, a touch of peaceful and glowing joy, without, however, loss of the greatness and sublimity that religious fragrance lends to culture and art.

49

One name brings this world of formative art before our eyes: Giotto. To a person who views the frescoes of Giotto, there is revealed a simple yet severe greatness, with a lovely sweetness and a sublime transfiguration that embody a closeness with nature and, in contrast to the archaic art of the Romantic Middle Ages, a loving regard for individual form. Yet it is the spirit of a chaste approach to nature that is far removed from naturalism. The individual and the concrete, however, already gain full attention, and this trend developed further throughout the Fourteenth and Fifteenth Centuries.

Who does not feel the close connection of this art with the spirit of St. Francis? We need not know that Giotto was a member of the Third Order of Penance to recognize and understand this close relationship. His works breathe the Franciscan spirit which did not only influence art greatly, but is itself pregnant with an artistic spirit, and liberates in man his artistic potentialities.

This is not the place to evaluate historically the tremendous influence of the Franciscan spirit on art, an influence that surpassed by far the range of the tertiaries and other religious orders as well. Whether the depth of the influence of the Franciscan spirit on the whole of the Fourteenth Century and on the unique flowering of art in the age of the Renaissance has been adequately appraised or not is a matter of debate. But we are above all concerned here with the affinity of the Franciscan spirit to creative art and to poetry.

Art is not simply the expression of the general spiritual attitude of the person. Art is a world all its own with standards peculiar to it. It is a reflection of the eternal beauty of God; for, God is the absolute Beauty, just as he is the absolute Goodness and Wisdom. Art has an intrinsic value, independent of its educational worth, or the joy it imparts. The artistic talent is a special gift of God; it cannot be defined any more than it can be traced back to its sources, be it sociological elements or other extraneous considerations; it is and remains a mystery. God speaks to us through every great work of art, even though the artist may not know God or submit himself to him. Still the artistic talent is not unrelated to the mentality and spirit of the individual and of the time in which he lives; it even presupposes certain basic attitudes in order that it may unfold properly. Some basic tendencies are inartistic in themselves; some times are deprived of any artistic sense. Certain approaches are required of a person in his relationship toward God and the world, if he is to become truly creative. Certain trends are presupposed at a particular time, if it is to be adorned with great art.

Here it is not so much a question of the theoretical *Weltanschauung* of the artist; rather it is a question of his existential, organic approach to God and to the world, whether he is fully conscious of it or not. Art presupposes an organic immediacy, at least a reverent basic attitude, an attitude which accepts objective values, for their own sake, independently of any possible use. The real artist has an unpragmatic spirit; with ears attuned, he catches the sound of the eternal in nature and in man, without however letting the narrowness of his individual life obstruct one's sensitiveness of soul.

The Franciscan spirit is an artistic spirit in a very special way. Its organic character, its directness, the absence in it of set purpose and design, are something specifically artistic. The principle of Catholicism that urges us to give

51

expression to what is interior and thus provides an objectivation and a final fulfillment acquires a special emphasis and expression in the Franciscan spirit. In whom was the longing for concrete expression felt more strongly and more deeply than in him who provided a real crib with living animals, an ox and an ass, in order that Christmas might be fittingly celebrated, and who sought to give intuitive, image-like expression to all forms of devotion?

This is the extreme opposite of that false gnostic mysticism that shuns everything clear and distinct and views every outward expression as a profanation and an alienation; this is the opposite of that false "interiorism" that identifies with depth the inexpressible and the stammered; a contrast to that spirit of pride that looks down upon the flesh and all visible creation, an attitude that marks the iconoclast of every age. It is also the opposite to seeing in the individual as such a degradation, an attitude proper to many oriental forms of pantheism. For Francis, who followed Christ literally, nothing was concrete enough; Francis found direct expression for everything; he walked through the woods singing aloud; he found a parting word for every rock on La Verna's heights; in him, all holy thoughts and acts found a unique, characteristic, visible expression of an exquisite charm and radiant loveliness. This extraordinary unity of interior life and exterior expression finds, as it were, a mysterious confirmation in the stigmata which he received on La Verna.

The Franciscan spirit is, as we already saw, uniquely poetical. The figure of St. Francis is encircled by a fragrance of enchanting sweetness; an intensely poetic atmosphere surrounds every movement, every situation of Francis' life. Picture the touching scene when Francis learned of the severity of life and the poverty of the brothers in Portugal. Overcome with joy, he rose and, turning toward the west, blessed the distant disciples with a great sign of the cross. What indescribable charm enveloped his every action! Every name he gave to creatures, every act he performed, every prayer he said, every song of praise he uttered, be it in his *Canticle of the Sun,* or his *Lauds,* everything reflected, not only the beauty we commonly see in every saint, but a beauty ånd graciousness that we find only in Francis. This poetic charm is indissolubly interwoven with his truly unique sanctity.

Nothing, therefore, is more erroneous than to interpret St. Francis only "lyrically," to set his sanctity in quotation marks, to describe his manner of conduct as poetic rather than to see the ultimate seriousness, the absolute reality and the exalted greatness of his life. He was a saint, and as a saint he must be understood. Every emphasis that subordinates his sanctity is intolerable and erroneous. This unique poetic charm can be rightly understood only by those who see his sanctity as an absolute value in itself, accepting it in its sublime seriousness without attempting any desubstantialization. One understands this clearly when one sees the lyricism that pervades the Francisan world of art, an art illuminated by the bright light of eternity, free of all shades and shadows, pure of all sultry sensuality, an art that is luminous and soaring.

With this we come to the second point, the specific style of Franciscan artistry. Francis' own *Canticle of the Sun,* the frescoes of Giotto, the poems of Thomas of Celano and of Jacopone da Todi, the *Fioretti,* all possess a light, soaring beauty that is specifically "classic." It is not a lovely land of fantasy that opens up to us, not a world of fairy tales, but it is a reflection of genuine reality of the world in its final, real, supernatural light. It is not a world that melts under the rays of the sun, whose charm escapes through one's fingers when it is seen in the light of eternity; but it is a world whose beauty is as clear as daylight, surrounded by an atmosphere that is distinctly eternal. This art has not the vital glow that comes from the rushing stream of life's fullness; it is a spiritual, super-vital art that is marked by a light and austere greatness, that is filled with heavenly peace and spiritual glow. It is not a spring of "vitality" which filled the Thirteenth and Fourteenth Centuries, nor the glorious bursting open of the plenitude of life in man; but it is a tender glow, a light that is transformed with joy, a gentle messenger of spring, a reflection of the resurrection, which the Church commemorates in spring. It is an exquisitely chaste art, humbly reflecting the world of values and showing the artist with bowed head and reverent gaze, contemplating the world as a creation of the eternal holy Lord. Nor is it an art that reflects the lonely greatness of genius, the searching struggle and tragedy of man who, driven by heroic yearning, looks out over the finite and limited world, but whose longing remains an anguished question which dies away in the universe. It is an art that is transformed by heavenly peace and rests in God.

It is an art that portrays supernatural harmony and is freed of all earthly concern and is filled with holy simplicity; an art in which tensions and conflicts are not ignored or artificially covered over, but are faced and solved.

Recall a verse of the *Dies Irae,* one of the truly great poems of all times and written probably by Thomas of Celano: *Rex tremendae majestatis, qui salvandos salvas gratis, salva me fons pietatis* ("King of dreaded majesty, who freely saves those to be saved, save me, O fount of kindness"). What is more admirable than the *Rex tremendae majestatis,* which expresses the fearful greatness of the living God; and the *fons pietatis* which stirs our hearts with the infinitely merciful meekness and love of God.

This art is not only a religious one; it is a specifically Christian, Catholic art, in which all is seen in Jesus and through Jesus, in which the world is brightened by the light of Jesus, the light that frees and transforms everything and basks in the splendor of him who said: "In the world, you will have affliction. But take courage, I have overcome the world" (Jn. 16, 33).

Who does not feel the deep inner relation of this art to the Franciscan spirit! It is not a question of subject matter, of presenting religious themes, or the frequent portrayal of St. Francis in some scene of his life; it is a matter of a much deeper relationship, namely, the influence of the Franciscan spirit on the world of art of that time. Whether a tree is painted or a distant landscape, all art creations give witness to the Franciscan spirit. When life is integrated in the Franciscan spirit, a specific artistic expression results and the works created diffuse the charm and beauty of heavenly light. The spirit of St. Francis shines resplendently like "the rainbow in the sky, like the budding rose in the spring time, like the lilies in flowing waters"; the sweetest sound of its spirit is the song that comes from the heart and resounds with the intoxicating sweetness of Jesus; a spirit whose every action blends the sublime and the lovely, the austere and the charming, the restful and the peaceful with the ringing and the startling, the last solemn earnestness with the peace and joy of the divine.

Yet the relation of Franciscanism to art is not restricted to the unheard of fecundation of art and poetry in the Trecento and Quattrocento. We are also confronted with the specific Franciscan beauty and charm in many Franciscan churches and friaries of later centuries. Whereas in the Trecento and Quattrocento, the very style of this art was Franciscan, the touching note of beauty also discloses itself in the Franciscan missions of San Luis Rey, or San Xavier del Bac, for instance, though historically speaking the style of Eighteenth Century architecture does not derive from Franciscanism.

But the combination of poverty, of a touching humility even in exterior appearance, and an intensity, warmth, and enchanting poetry impresses us especially in the interior of San Xavier del Bac. It has the same spirit as the unique refectory of St. Clare in San Damiano in Assisi, where greatest poverty and simplicity are combined with a heart-melting beauty.

In the lives of many other saints great reforms were intended, great achievements even in many social and cultural domains were intentionally accomplished. St. Francis on the contrary sought nothing else than the literal imitation of Christ. He wanted only one thing: to follow Christ in everything and to be the most faithful, obedient son of the Church. He intended none of the various deep changes which he *de facto* brought about. Indeed, in St. Francis, we find the fulfillment of the word of our Lord: "Seek first the kingdom of God and his justice, and all these things shall be given you besides" (Mt. 6, 33).

II

Come, Follow Me

"If you wish to enter into life, keep the commandments. . . . If you wish to be perfect, go, sell what you have, and give to the poor, and you shall have treasure in heaven; and come, follow me"
(Matt 19.17, 21).

4

Following Christ
in the World

"If you wish to enter into life, keep the Commandments
. . . If you wish to be perfect, go, sell what you have and
give to the poor, and you shall have treasure in heaven;
and come, follow me" (Mt. 19, 17 and 21).

With these words our Lord and Savior, Jesus Christ,
points out two ways: the ordinary, which requires the mini-
mum for salvation; and the more austere and higher way,
which leads to perfection. Are there then two ways that lead
to heaven? Do we not read. "Who dares climb the mountain
of the Lord, and appear in his sanctuary? The guiltless in
act, the pure in heart" (Ps. 23, 3). Surely only he who
denies himself and follows Christ can gain eternal happiness; only he who is born again in Christ, he whose nature
is transformed by grace, only he who has recognized in his

glory, Jesus, "full of grace and truth, the Son of the Father," he who has become a living member of his holy, infallible Church can reach the City of God, the "heavenly Jerusalem." And yet there are two ways.

The evangelical counsels constitute the way of perfection: poverty, chastity, and obedience. Not only evil desire and pride are to be resisted—that must be done by everyone who keeps the commandments; but even a lawful concern about earthly things and a legitimate sense of independence are to be subdued and removed. The right to lawful goods, the right to possess, the right to marry, the right to determine freely for oneself in extramoral domains. This is the steep and thorny way and is undoubtedly, as a state of life, the higher one; but this way requires a specific call.

Yet, is the goal of perfection possible only on this heroic way that the "strong group" of monks or friars and brides of Christ pursue? Is it possible only among that supernatural family, founded by saints, and producing saints, and overcoming corruptions that now and then creep in, that family that "shall flourish like the palm tree, and shall grow like the cedar of Lebanon"? "They who are planted in the house of the Lord shall flourish in the courts of the Lord" (cf Ps. 91, 13); their whole way of life, from the rule of the order to the habit that is worn, proclaims victory over the world,—"that is our Faith"; their existence alone is already a sign of the divinity of the Church to him who sees with open eyes. Are these religious the only ones who strive after perfection and who are not satisfied with the keeping of the commandments, who in holy persistence "never cease to knock"?

Their way is indeed the more perfect way, but it is not

the only way. There is also a way of life in the world, along which the same degree of transformation into Christ, that is, perfection, can be sought after. I am not thinking of individuals whom God chooses as special vessels of grace, whom the Lord "loves and adorns," whom the Lord invests with "the garment of glory." "The spirit of God moves where it wills"; God can raise saints among the members of his Church, in and out of the cloister, for to each person is given the opportunity to die to self and to be wholly reborn in Christ through the merciful streams of grace that flow from the side of Christ, the means of grace that branch out like so many rays from the light of the world, the light that is Jesus, the light that is reflected in the face of the Holy Virgin and all the saints, even though the individual is in the midst of the world, yet "born not of blood, nor of the will of the flesh, nor of the will of man, but of God" (Jn. 1, 13). No, our question is: Is there a way of following Christ totally outside the cloister, a way of life set down in a rule whereby the same transformation in Christ can be attained? Does the spirit of breaking with the world and going beyond what is strictly demanded find some form of life outside the cloister?

We find such ways of life throughout all the centuries in the Church: The Oblates of St. Benedict, the thirteen Third Orders, and today also many religious communities of lay people, striving for a full surrender to Christ, a full transformation into Christ. These lay communities seek to unite by means of a simple rule of life all those who, though they remain in the world, wish to be free of every attachment to the world and wish not only to seek first the kingdom of God, as all Christians are bound to do, but wish also to live the Christian life in all its fulness and richness.

The essential difference between the life of the ordinary Christian and the life of one who seeks to follow Christ more closely can be found by asking these questions: Is Jesus for us only the Lord, Redeemer, and Judge, or is he also one's Spouse and Beloved, for whom one's soul yearns as the deer pants after the fountain of living water, looking to Jesus not only with deep reverence and the firm will to keep his commandments, but also with the loving desire to be united with Christ saying with St. John: *"Veni Jesu Domine."* This is what determines whether one wants merely to keep the commandments or whether one wants to reach a full surrender of oneself to Christ.

This is the higher state of transformation, the state of perfection, the freedom from earthly cares, and the continuous turning towards Jesus Christ, "the Crucified," whom "to serve is to reign"; when Jesus is the center of life, when to follow him and to renounce the world is life's ambition, when from him and in him all things take their meaning—this is the life of the Oblates and the various Third Orders for those who remain in the world and do not profess the evangelical counsels.

A Third Order is an order for the people in the world who indeed keep their role as parent or spouse, as businessman or farmer, but in such a manner that everything is restored in Christ, according to the saintly tertiary pope, St. Pius X's word, *"instaurare omnia in Christo."* They should break with the spirit of the world as genuinely as do the religious; they should serve Jesus, the King of eternal glory; they should center their lives in Jesus, over and above what is demanded of every Christian; and they should rest in Jesus, and be able to say with St. Francis, "My God and my all." All these forms of striving for perfection outside the convent, share not only this goal with the religious orders, but also the element of community. It is not the effort of an individual but always of a community, a group which the individual joins. Therefore, the oblates, as well as the Third Orders have a rule, which prescribes at least the pattern of the way on which the individual member tries to follow Christ more closely.

Community has a high value of its own. It is not only a help for the individual in his striving for perfection, but, in itself, it glorifies God, it is a victory of Christ, who has said: "Where two or more are gathered together in my name I shall be in the midst of them." That communion with other persons in Christ is not only a means to attain our eternal goal, but a great good in itself, is clearly disclosed by the fact that there is a *communio sanctorum* in eternity, that the beatific vision cannot be severed from an ultimate union with all the other persons who attain this vision. Though, in eternity, communion has no longer the function of helping us to attain eternal welfare, it has an infinite value, as indicated in the prayer of our Lord: *"Ut unum sint."*

We must understand that already on earth communion in Christ, a community which is rooted in Christ, in which one encounters one another in Christ, embodies a new dimension of glorification of God, with respect to the sanctification of the individual. Certainly the glorification through the sanctification of the individual is still more important and essential. But one must understand that in the community rooted in Christ, something is added, that one dimension of the kingdom of God can only be realized through the community in Christ. Thus we find a twofold role of community in religious orders. First, the community is a great help to the individual in his striving for perfection. The very fact that this effort is made in common, and that a community life is filled with a sacred atmosphere, draws the individual always again to God, forms a continuous *sursum corda* (lift up your hearts). Secondly, the very existence of such a community is a victory of Christ and has a high value of its own.

Who does not feel that the love of Jesus, who once said, "Where two are gathered in my name, there am I in the midst of them," unites all in a supernatural love? Who does not feel that the loving union of two souls in Jesus, who said, "This is my commandment that you love one another," is a part of the genuine adoration of God and the true imitation of Christ? The more intimate and continuous the following of Christ is, the more intimate and real will be the supernatural union of all Christ's followers, especially those who walk the same way toward the kingdom of God. One sacrifice, one faith, one Church, one fold, and one Shepherd, who urged us to say, "Our Father," and not "My Father." What could be pleasing to God if it did not flow from the spirit of him who said, "Be one in the love of the Father"; if it were not in harmony with the spirit of the spouse of Christ, holy Church, in which through liturgical prayer waves of streaming love ascend to God, coming from many hearts, like an eternal *Gloria Patri et Filio et Spiritui Sancto* (Glory be to the Father and to the Son and to the Holy Spirit).

It is therefore understandable that also among those who want to strive for perfection in the world, we find not only individuals but groups and communities. Though here a community life in the strict sense is out of the question, though the members of these communities have their own

64

private life, the character of a common effort remains a great help for the individual and the community possesses the character of a victory of Christ.

We may say: the Third Orders and all similar groups of persons, who want to follow Christ unconditionally in the world, share two things with the religious orders: the desire to give oneself totally to Christ and the element of community. If they are affiliated to some religious orders, such as the Oblates and the different Third Orders, they also will be inspired by the individual note of piety of the respective religious order to which they are affiliated.

The effort to accomplish a full donation of oneself to Christ in the world was, in former times, mostly linked to a religious order. The Oblates are affiliated to an individual Benedictine monastery, the Third Orders to the Franciscan, Dominican, Carmelite orders, etc. Today, on the contrary, we find many religious groups of lay people striving for perfection in the world, which have no such affiliation to a religious order. Yet it must be stressed that in any case, whether such an affiliation exists or not, the following of Christ in the world is not intended as a simple copy of the life of the monks, or friars, but as a genuine life in the world, though not in the spirit of the world.

Those who strive for perfection in the world, have obviously another vocation than the religious. St. Louis of France was called to be a perfect King and a perfect husband; had he acted as if he were a friar, he would not have lived up to his specific vocation. Not only are the tasks of a different nature, but the duty to fulfill these tasks as well as possible also belongs to their vocation; also their relation to various natural goods must be of another kind. The fact that the way of the evangelical counsels, as such, is the more perfect one, should not induce the members of a Third Order to copy the religious as much as possible, and to become, as it were, "disguised monks or friars." The superiority of the status of a monk or friar is no reason for believing that the transformation in Christ of the individual soul could not take place equally within the framework of a group striving for perfection in the world.

It is of the utmost importance that the two vocations be clearly distinguished and the life of the non-religious be not regarded in the light of a half-religious vocation, of a kind of antechamber of the religious order. The one who wants to follow Christ unconditionally in the world, should not take the attitude of the monk or friar as a pattern, because it belongs to his very vocation to act and behave differently upon many occasions. They have definitely another task, they have to accomplish the *instaurare omnia in Christo,* with respect to many goods, from which the religious has turned away. But notwithstanding the essential difference between the religious groups striving for perfection in the world, and the religious orders, the name of "Third Order" remains fully justified. Because all the religious groups striving for perfection in the world, whether oblates, or the various Third Orders differ essentially from all the pious associations or fraternities.

All of these associations and fraternities do not totally engage their members; they do not imply a total commitment of the individual, that is, the beginning of a new life, a turning away from the "pomp of the world," a total surrender to Christ. In becoming a member of these associations, one commits oneself to certain prayers, to certain financial contributions, to certain duties concerning the association. But joining these associations does not imply a *conversio morum*. It is, therefore, characteristic of these associations, that in them one finds no investiture, no novitiate, no profession.

Moreover, all these pious associations are dedicated to a specific concrete end, for instance, to help the missions, to fight obscene literature, or whatever religious aim it may be; confraternities are mostly united by a specific devotion, whereas neither the oblates nor the Third Orders have such a special end. Their end is the full transformation in Christ.

Finally the role of the end differs strikingly in both cases. The pious associations are means for attaining an extrinsic pious end. The end of the groups striving for perfection in the world, on the contrary, is the *forma* of these communities, the name in which they are united. This fact has a bearing on the very nature of the structure of the respective communities.

Indeed, membership in a Third Order implies a *conversio morum,* a rebirth of the whole man. And so the priest prays as he is about to invest the postulant: "May the Lord divest you of the old man with his acts, and turn away your heart from the pomps of the world, which you renounced when you received baptism."

5

The Layman's Order
of Saint Francis

Among the Third Orders the best known and most widely propagated is that of St. Francis—the Third Order of Penance.* We do not claim that all the fraternities of the Third Order in our epoch incorporate the features which characterize the Third Order as such. A tendency in human nature to slacken one's pace or to replace the spirit of a highly religious way of life by the letter can be observed again and again in the course of history.

The ardor, the zeal of the first time, the full understanding of the intentions of the holy founder of an order tend to fade after a certain time. Thus after a while, a need for reforms usually becomes apparent, reforms in the sense of renewal, both of the original ardor, and the absolute character of its intentions. But the possibility of this renewal

69

*Note: The 1978 promulgation of a new rule of life changed the order's name from the Third Order of Penance (Secular) to the Secular Franciscan Order.

after the decay in a religious order testifies to the inexhaustible youth of the supernatural life. We only need think of St. Bernardin of Siena, to see such rejuvenation of the authentic Franciscan life.

If the danger of slackening threatens the traditional religious order, the danger of losing the original spirit is even much greater in all types of Third Orders or oblates. The fact that they remain in the world and are not continually reminded of their vocation by their surroundings, exposes them much more to the rhythm of slackening, so deeply rooted in human nature, and of losing the original spirit, the original idea of the Third Order.

So much less is required to enter the Third Order than to become a monk or friar. When a person enters a monastic order, a clear-cut incision in his daily life takes place inasmuch as everything takes place under the vigilant eyes of the master of novices and the superior. This is not to be found in the Third Order, and thus it is understandable that the Third Orders lose their authentic character, their original impact, more easily with the passing of time, unless a renewal is accomplished in a particular fraternity by its spiritual director.

It may thus well be that someone, upon entering the Third Order, gets the impression that our picture of the Third Order is incorrect. He may argue, "I have not observed any difference between the Third Order and any pious association or confraternity such as you claim exists between them." To this we must answer: Yes indeed, often the Third Order is handled by its director and lived by its members in a way which makes it completely equal to any pious association or confraternity. But this is no argument against the difference which exists between the Third Order as such and a pious association, which will always be found if the fraternity of tertiaries remains faithful to the original spirit of the Third Order. In order to know what the Third Order really means, what was the idea of St. Francis in establishing the Third Order, we should think of the Third Order at the time of Blessed Lucchesio da Poggibonsi, St. Elizabeth of Hungary, or St. Louis of France. If we want to understand the true nature of something we should always look at examples in which this nature is fully developed, and not at incomplete and inadequate representatives. Thus our interpretation of the Third Order should be understood as an elaboration of what the Third Order should be and what it has *de facto* been originally.

Oftentimes in the liturgy, we find the following prayer: "that . . . we may learn to despise earthly things and to love those of heaven" (*terrena despicere, et amare caelestia*).

Obviously the term *"terrena,"* "earthly," does not refer to evil and sinful things. Earthly is not the antithesis to morally good. "Earthly things" refer rather to things which are not sinful in themselves, but which are opposed as "earthly" to "heavenly things." It would, however, be just as wrong to identify "earthly" with natural. The fact that the prayer suggests that we should despise "earthly" things indicates that we must still distinguish between earthly and natural goods.

There are many natural goods which we should never despise, such as beauty in nature or art, truth in philosophy and science, and above all friendship and marriage. It is thus of the utmost importance to clarify the meaning of "earthly" in this context.

From the very beginning we must exclude any illegitimate good, or anything which is subjectively satisfying only because of its appeal to our pride or concupiscence. But among legitimate objective goods for the person, we must distinguish between those which are objective goods for us because of their value and those which are good merely because of their agreeableness. To the first type of objective goods belong beauty in art and nature, truth in philosophy, or friendship, marriage, any artistic gift, and any noble talent granted to us; whereas good food, wealth, an influential position, fame, honors—all these delight us, not because of their value, but because they are agreeable to us.

All the goods which are bearers of values reflect God, the Infinite Goodness, Beauty, and Holiness, in their value. They are natural goods, certainly, but they are not "worldly" goods. Granted that every created good can be abused, that we can approach any created good in such a way that it becomes a danger for us, there is still an essential difference between those goods which have as such a kind of "worldly" character, and those natural goods which in no way have this character, but which rather point to a "world above," and a reality beyond this world. These tell us something of God and of heaven. Though earthly in the sense that they are in their present form relative to our earthly existence, these goods nonetheless are resplendent with a value carrying a message from above; if we rightly understand their meaning, they draw us into the depth of our soul and increase our thirst for the heavenly goods.

If we emphasize this distinction between worldly goods and earthly ones among natural goods, we certainly do not wish to minimize the difference between the most noble earthly goods and the heavenly ones. One cannot stress enough the completely new and unique character of the supernatural world, of the quality of holiness, with respect to the highest natural values. This difference is emphasized when St. Paul says: *"Quae sursum sunt quaerite, non quae sunt in terra."* Nevertheless, the distinction between "worldly" and "earthly" among natural goods is of fundamental importance for Christian life. The attitude of the true Christian to the "worldly" and to the non-worldly natural goods, which are however earthly and not heavenly, should be a very different one. The Christian should not seek wordly goods, and when they are bestowed upon him, without his having striven for them, he should *use* them, remaining aware of the danger which they include, aware that as soon as we start enjoying them for their own sake, they are prone to thwart our full concentration on Christ. Because in the very quality of these goods, there is an antithesis to the supernatural world, their "worldly" character makes it impossible to yearn for them without some alienation from Christ.

Natural goods endowed with a high value, on the contrary, call for another response. Their value, when rightly understood, has the character of a message of God, a reflection of his infinite beauty; and, thus, an enjoyment of them for their own sake, our praying for them, need not be incompatible with the full desire for heavenly goods. Later on, we shall see which are the presuppositions for the compatibility of these goods with a fully religious life. Detachment from "worldly" goods is common to all those who want to follow Christ unconditionally. But it is with respect to those non-worldly natural goods, that we find two different ways of dealing in the history of the Church.

There is a noble, rugged way, by which one frees oneself in a heroic fashion not only from all earthly goods, but even closes one's eyes to their beauty and charm, as one reflects on earth's transitoriness, echoed in the word, "Vanity of vanities and all is vanity." One avoids becoming engrossed in genuine natural goods in order to be completely free for the highest Good, the essence of all beauty; one becomes blind and deaf to the good and beautiful that is earthly, to be free for the eternal, for "the old and new beauty" of the "King of eternal glory." One realizes how small the earth is and begins to appreciate how immense heaven is.

It is the way the great Fathers of the desert pursued relentlessly, the way that existed at all times in the Church, from the times of St. Anthony of the Desert to the times of St. John of the Cross who demands complete renunciation to all earthly goods.

But there is also a way in which these authentic earthly —yet not worldly—goods become steps to God on account of their authentic value; in which they are viewed in the light of Christ, as coming from the goodness of God, grasping them in their original meaning as intended by God in creating them. This way is also to be found in the life of the Church throughout the centuries.

Perhaps this difference between the two ways of Christian perfection, mentioned by Abbot Butler in his book *Benedictine Monachism,* comes to the fore in a striking way if we compare the story of a father of the desert with the one of St. Benedict's visit to St. Scholastica.

The sister of a desert father wrote to him that she had but one desire before her imminent death: to see her brother. He refused to come. The bishop, however, ordered him to visit his sister. The desert father obeyed, and went to the house of his sister; while remaining on the street, he called her saying: "You wanted to see me, here I am; look at me quickly that I may go." As soon as his sister approached the window, he closed his eyes, and left immediately without exchanging another word with her.

The attitude of this desert father forms a radical contrast to the one of St. Benedict and St. Scholastica. When darkness was setting in, they took their meal together and continued their conversation at table until it was quite late. Then the holy nun said to him: "Please do not leave me tonight, brother. Let us keep on talking about the joys of heaven till morning." "What are you saying, sister?" he replied. "You know I cannot stay away from the monastery."

The sky was so clear at the time, there was not a cloud in sight. At her brother's refusal, Scholastica folded her hands on the table and rested her head upon them in earnest prayer. When she looked up again, there was a sudden burst of lightning and thunder, accompanied by such a downpour that Benedict and his companions were unable to set foot outside the door. . . .

Realizing that he could not return to the abbey in this terrible storm, Benedict complained bitterly. "God forgive you, sister!" he said. "What have you done?"

Scholastica simply answered: "When I appealed to you, you would not listen to me. So I turned to my God and he heard my prayer. Leave now if you can. Leave me here and go back to your monastery."

This of course, he could not do. He had no choice now but to stay, in spite of his unwillingness. They spent the entire night together and both of them derived great profit from the holy thoughts they exchanged about the interior life. (Taken from St. Gregory the Great's *Life and Miracles*

75

of St. Benedict, newly translated by Odo J. Zimmermann O.S.B. and Benedict R. Avery O.S.B., pp. 6-69.)

The importance granted by God to holy love, clearly illustrated in this episode, is confirmed by the liturgy: *"Plus potuit a Deo quia plus amavit"* (She obtained more from God, because she loved more").

It is obvious that the evangelical counsels imply a turning away not only from "worldly," but also from several high natural, non-worldly goods, such as marriage. But the sacrifice of this high natural good, implied in the specific vocation of religious life, certainly does not carry with it a despising of this good. The difference of attitudes to be found in the Church with respect to high natural goods, extends therefore also to religious life.

This positive way was realized in a special manner in the life of St. Francis, as we saw before. Thus the eyes of the tertiary should be fully open to all true natural values; these should be seen in their innermost beauty which discloses itself only when approached in the light of supernature. Then, they truly become windows for God's beauty; they are recognized as vessels of God's superabundant bounty and infinite love.

The beauty and goodness of earthly (not-worldly) goods should be deeply appreciated, since they all come from God, the "Father of light." One drinks deeply of the value of all things when one views them supernaturally, when one sees how they reach toward the infinite and reflect the beauty of God, whose goodness and glory are made manifest through them. But one thereby misses in no way their natural splendor and delight, because supernature neither destroys nature, nor changes it, but perfects it.

The essential precondition for this approach to natural,

yet non-worldly goods, is, however, the primacy of the *caelestia*. It is the full response to the unique quality of holiness of the infinite, sacred beauty of the Godman. It is the *sensus supranaturalis,* the enchantment by the splendor of holiness, which forced the apostles to follow Christ *relictis omnibus*. It is the longing for this world of the supernatural, which must have the primacy. And only he who possesses this attitude can see the great, natural goods in their ultimate beauty in Christ; only he can *instaurare omnia in Christo.*

Today one often hears the praise of natural goods voiced also by Catholics. One stresses the importance of work, one says "working also is prayer if it is done with the right intention," one praises the growing mastership of man over nature. This attitude toward natural goods, however, is in no way the one we are advocating here, the one which should characterize the tertiary. He who says: "You do not need to pray so much; your work is prayer," forgets that our work can attain a pray-like character only if we grant to prayer, in the literal sense, its full place in our life. So those who praise natural goods by giving them a place besides the supernatural in no way do justice to these goods. They forget that only when these goods are seen in the light of Christ, in their exaltation through Christ, can they unfold their highest value and deserve to play a role in the life of the Christian, who wants to give himself completely to Christ.

The role which these high natural goods should play in the life of a Christian can neither be detached from the fact that the supernatural goods have a primacy, nor from the fact that these goods must be seen in the light of Christ, even in their transformation through Christ.

The modern emphasis of certain Catholics on natural goods is a way of life in which our hearts are not touched by God's supernatural glory; our hearts do not long for the "courts of the Lord, our God"; one is apt to consider God merely as a guide in life's ways. No, the Franciscan way is not a half-hearted break with the "spirit" of the world. It excludes in no way a full giving of oneself to Christ.

Perhaps this is even a deeper separation from the spirit of the world than the austere, above-mentioned way, of following Christ, for here the heart is so aflame with love of Jesus, that all natural goodness and beauty are seen as coming from him, the source of all goodness and beauty; when instead of turning away indiscriminately from all created goods, the distinction between the worldly goods with their siren song and their poisoned sweetness and the true natural goods is made. Then the earth becomes, as it were, transparent; one clearly grasps the ultimate link between every true value and God; one meets Christ in every true good, and thus never abandons the *"religio"* to God. Then all true goods become a message from God and enable us to see everything in the light of the one event of all events, before which the angels and archangels tremble: *"et incarnatus est de Spiritu Sancto ex Maria Virgine et homo factus est."*

We saw in the last chapter that neither the oblates nor any kind of tertiary should have the character of "disguised" monks or friars. Certainly, they should accomplish the same total surrender to Christ; they should follow Christ with the same seriousness; and they also should turn away from the "spirit" of the world and from worldly things. But they should not simply copy the religious, though remaining in the world; they should not turn away from the world as monks and friars do.

Nevertheless, their way of following Christ will also reflect the specific individual note of the religious order to whom they are affiliated, or they will be inspired by the individual note of the founder of this order. Thus we can say that the Third Order of St. Francis strives for perfection in the Franciscan way. As they strive for sanctity with the same ardor as the friars, what marks the true Friar Minor must be the mark of distinction also for the disciple of St. Francis in his Third Order. As much as their way of life should differ from the one of the friars, the *virtues* which they are eager to attain are the same. Thus he is a true tertiary who imitates the virtues of the early members of the First Order; the faithfulness of Brother Bernard, who showed his sincerity most perfectly in his love of poverty; the simplicity and purity of Brother Leo, who was a man of the greatest purity; the courtliness of Brother Angelo, who was the first knight to enter the order and who showed courtliness and goodness on every occasion; the pleasant manners and charming graciousness of speech of Brother Masseo, the lofty spirit of contemplation of Brother Giles; the intense activity of Brother Rufino, who prayed without ceasing and was always intimately united with God; the nearly perfect patience of Brother Juniper, who kept the course of righteousness before his eyes and longed to follow Christ on the way of the cross; the physical and spiritual strength of Brother John, who was the strongest man physically of his time; the love of Brother Roger whose life was all aglow with love; the solicitous care of Brother Lucido who was most thoughtful and considerate of others and who did not want to stay even one month in any one place, but went from place to place, for, as he said: "We have a lasting dwelling place, not here, but only in heaven." Yet the two saints who perhaps are the most typical pattern for the tertiaries are St. Louis of France and St. Elizabeth of Hungary, because in them we find a specific example of sanctity in the world. In their unique love for their spouses, we clearly grasp the difference between their way of life and the one lived in a religious order.

Not many receive the grace to follow this way to its fullest extent; but to the extent that they do become fools for Christ and trample under foot the world and all its worldly maxims, they conquer the world, in the world, and become true sons of St. Francis.

The face of the earth was renewed by the Third Order in the Thirteenth and Fourteenth Centuries. Consider the life of Blessed Angela of Foligno, of St. Elizabeth of Hungary, of St. Louis IX, of St. Rose of Viterbo, of St. Ferdinand of Castile, of St. Elizabeth of Portugal. Who does not think of the words of Jesus, the source of life and holiness, "I am the vine, you are the branches." Look at the number of those who came with no weapons into a world at war; who opposed the might of the world with the strength of weakness; who in a world of softness and debauchery wore the garment of penance; who opposed the pomp of the world with the poverty of Christ; who in a time of class struggle, of oppression and injustice, united people of all walks of life, from king to beggar, as brothers in Christ, disdaining the world and its maxims; who united in a victorious love above the continual battles of cities and nations; who as members of Christ's Mystical Body came as an army of peace-makers; who overcame the world by becoming fools for Christ within the world.

They did this as true sons and daughters of St. Francis,

of whom we read the following story:

The first knowledge Francis acquired of the home relations was, that the podesta and bishop were in open strife, and that the bishop had placed the ban upon the podesta and the podesta in return had forbidden all citizens to have anything to do with the bishop. "It is a great shame for us, God's servants," said Francis to his Brothers, "that no one makes peace here." And to do what he could he composed two new verses for his Sun Song, and then sent a messenger to the podesta to come to the bishop's residence, and one to the bishop to meet him. The summoned ones came and gathered together on the Piazza del Vescovado—the same place where, nineteen years before, Francis had given back his clothes to his father. And when all were there, two Friars Minor stepped out and sang the first Sun Song, as Francis had originally written it, and then the new verses:

"Praised be you, O Lord, for those who give pardon
    for your love
and endure infirmity and tribulation;
blessed those, who endure in peace,
who will be, Most High, crowned by you."

Whilst the two Brothers sang, all stood with folded hands, as if the Gospel was being read in church. But when the song was ended, and the last *Laudato si Mi signore* had ceased to be heard, the podesta made a step forward, cast himself down before Bishop Guido and said: "Out of love to our Lord Jesus Christ and to his servant Francis, I forgive you from my heart and am ready to do your will, as it may seem good to you."

But the Bishop leaned over and drew up his enemy, em-

81

braced him and kissed him and said: "On account of my office I should be humble and peaceful. But I am by nature inclined to anger, and you must therefore be indulgent with me."

But the Brothers went in and told Francis of the victory he had won over the evil spirits of dissension with his song (Joergensen, pp. 322-323).

The Third Order will be able to change again the face of the earth only if it returns to its true greatness, to its sublime vocation, to its great responsibility; only if it gathers under the banner of Christ those who choose the spirit of St. Francis as their goal and say with St. Francis, "My love is crucified." The Third Order is not a group of admirers of St. Francis; it is a community, an order, that opposes the spirit of the world in the Franciscan way. It is made up of those who accept these words of Jesus, "If anyone wishes to come after me, let him deny himself, and take up his cross, and follow me" (Mt. 16, 24), and who cherish these words in their hearts. And to those true tertiaries St. Francis says: "And I, in the name of God, promise you eternal life, if you observe all these things; in the name of the Father and of the Son and of the Holy Spirit. Amen."

6

The Franciscan
Third Order Today

One sometimes hears the question: "Has the Third Order anything to offer to our present epoch?"

This very question indicates that the nature of the Third Order has not been understood at all. As we have stressed time and again, the Third Order does not pursue a special end, such as the care of the poor and sick, or the liberation of captives; but it strives exclusively for "the one thing necessary," the one goal of our conversion and sanctification. And the importance of this goal is in no way altered by any of the changes which take place in the course of history.

This independence from any historical epoch applies not only to the purpose of the Franciscan Third Order—an aim which it shares with all Third Orders, as well as with the Benedictine Oblates—but also to the specific character of the Third Order of Penance, that is of the Franciscan piety which characterizes it. For the individual note which distinguishes the Benedictine, the Dominican, the Carmelite, or the Franciscan way is not only the result of specific cultural surroundings or a specific epoch of history. These different ways leading to the same goal are all individual, valid forms of piety, which fit into every epoch. They testify to the variety of the ways of following Christ as well as to the absolute unity in the final end, and to the spirit of Christ living in them. The difference in question does not refer to different epochs, but to the differences between individuals, who can be found in every epoch. In any historical epoch, many may be called to follow the Benedictine way, and many the Franciscan way. Consequently, the difference in the individual personality of the holy founder which is expressed in the specific form of piety of his order, will remain a valid way for certain individuals at all times of history, and will lead to the one goal common to all.

The Franciscan way is a classical form, bearing the imprint of eternity and has, therefore, a specific message to give to all different epochs of history. Out of its supernatural plenitude it includes a response to all the typical dangers of any epoch.

The Third Order of Penance, far from being superannuated in our epoch, is thus still a way toward overcoming the specific dangers of our time.

In contemplating the personality of St. Francis, the striking contrast to the aberrations of the modern man cannot be overlooked. It is as if he emanated a light which mercilessly unmasks all the perversions of our epoch, yet simultaneously gives to our soul wings through his holy joy and ultimate freedom, thus filling us with the hope and the courage to fight the dangers of our times. His ultimate reverence and humility, the deep radiant joy filling his soul, a joy which is indissolubly linked to the full acceptance of man's creaturehood, throws the insanity of the modern alleged autarchy, the refusal to admit any bond or obligation, into sharp relief. On the one hand, there is the luminous humility of St. Francis; on the other, the insipid modern pride. On the one side, we find the true inner freedom, the freedom of the children of God, the victorious freedom which is a fruit of the total surrender to Christ; on the other hand, the slavery of the one who denies any obligation and follows his impulses indiscriminately.

Can a greater contrast to the dull, gray conception of the universe which we called "the laboratory view" be imagined than the luminous, rich world which was reality for St. Francis? Is the sight of the universe of St. Francis, for whom all creatures and their colorful splendor were understood in their valid reality, to such an extent that he addressed them and invited them to a common praise of God, not the most radical antithesis to the blindness of those who believe that the only valid reality is the one which is accessible to natural science? The one whose heart has been touched by St. Francis will thus be not only especially protected from the fatal error of the laboratory idol, but he will also be endowed with the spiritual gifts to heal those who have fallen prey to this superstition.

St. Francis is the epitome of the holy independence which is the radical antithesis to all brands of human respect. His unique originality testifies to his complete independence from all conventions, and from all standards

85

imposed by the public opinion of a certain epoch. He who has been awakened by St. Francis and has "tasted" his spirit, will be especially immunized against the infection of modern trends.

In order to resist the trends of a certain epoch, a special effort is necessary. Great is the power of trends, which are, as it were, in the air; great is for many the fascination connected with the notion of "modern," of corresponding to our present epoch. Great is the temptation to strive for "being up to date," even for those who do not consciously worship "being up to date." These trends in the air constitute a danger because they enter, as it were, through our pores; they influence us, even if we do not expressly commit ourselves to them. Great is the danger of uniformism; it is especially great in our present epoch and in the United States. The tertiary should be fully aware of this danger and consciously fight against it. The true tertiary should not be formed by the spirit of the epoch; the question whether something is "modern," up to date, should play no role for him. Christ is for him the only Master. The tertiary should judge everything from the point of view whether it can stand the test before Christ, whether it is compatible with Christ. He is thus neither conservative nor progressive. As Christ is the denominator of his life, he will follow St. Paul's admonition: "Test everything; retain what is good."

Every Catholic should see the great and mysterious natural goods—which also reflect God's glory and also contain a message of God, in their deepest meaning and value, and in the splendor they receive through their transfiguration in Christ. A mediocre, humdrum approach to those goods, be it the beauty of nature, be it man as such, created after the image of God, be it friendship, be it love, be it marriage, is a refusal to testify to the new light which Christ has shed on the entire creation.

It has been said that Christians are to be recognized by the fact that they love one another; we could add: Christians should also be recognized by the fact that they who have received the festive clothes in baptism, shun any superficial, mediocre approach to the great goods of creation, that they understand more profoundly than others *"quam admirabilia sunt opera tua Domine"* (How admirable are your works O God).

The tertiary, however, who wants to be a spiritual son or daughter of St. Francis, is especially called to testify to this deep vision of the universe, and to the new light which Christ has shed on creation. Consequently he will be particularly equipped to counteract the corrosion of nature which, as we saw, takes place today, especially in the relation between the two sexes, in the blunt amorality of those who have lost all sense for the mystery of sex; he will testify to the view of sex expressed in the beautiful prayer:

"O Lord our God, who created man pure and spotless and thereafter ordain that in the propagation of the human race one generation should be produced from another by the mystery of sweet love. . . ."

The Franciscan ideal of poverty is an antithesis to the widespread modern conception of happiness. Many believe that comfort is the very condition for true happiness. To have a refrigerator, a washing machine seems to them an indispensable presupposition for a happy human life. The tertiary inspired by the Franciscan ideal of poverty will understand that this notion of happiness contains a great error. While not refusing any such exterior help when bestowed on him, he will clearly see how secondary comfort is and how many dangers of pampering ourselves lie hidden in it. This applies above all to letting ourselves go, that is to the ideal of formless demeanor mentioned above. The Franciscan spirit of poverty is also incompatible with this kind of self-indulgence. St. Francis is not only the most illustrative example of how the greatest poverty can go hand in hand with a glorious form, but also of how an extraordinary spontaneity is compatible with the absence of all self-indulgence.

We saw how the exterior demeanor of St. Francis portrayed his deep reverence, humility, and an extreme severity toward his own body. He is certainly a striking antithesis to any form of self-indulgence. His very face—whether we think of the early painting in Subiaco or of the portrait in the fresco of Cimabue in San Francesco in Assisi, breathes a noble spirituality, a holy sobriety and self-control, and simultaneously an extraordinary spontaneity.

Seeing everything in the light of Christ, guided by the spirit of St. Francis, the tertiary will not be caught in the illusion of progressivism, nor will he confuse natural ideals with the Christian spirit. He will clearly grasp the abyss which yawns between the ideal of "equality" in the French Revolution, and the supernatural unity expressed in the words: *"Congregavit nos in unum Christi amor."* The spirit of St. Francis will help him to develop a "supernatural sense." The tertiary will thus not be caught by the widespread error of seeing an ideal in a pluralism of *Weltanschauungen*. He will, on the contrary, see in it an evil, but one which we must accept as a cross. He will not see an expression of the plenitude of life in pluralism, but rather a consequence of original sin. He will certainly understand

88

that this pluralism cannot be overcome by force, that it can only be fought by spiritual weapons. The true tertiary will be aware that true tolerance is in no way equivalent with considering all convictions and creeds as being equally valuable. He clearly sees that truth is by its very nature not pluralistic, but exclusive. Tolerance only means that one should not impose truth upon another person by force, but it certainly does not imply that we should not try to convince the other person, and ardently wish that he should find Christ.

The Third Order invites us to follow the admonition of St. Augustine: "Kill the error; love the one who errs." The true tertiary will understand that the killing of the error is an essential part of the love of neighbor, because his errors are the greatest evil *for him;* in fact I cannot love him without ardently desiring his conversion.

The spirit of St. Francis, who did not shun the greatest strains and dangers in order to reach the sultan in Egypt and try to convert him, is certainly a radical contrast to those who see in "pluralism" an ideal and a sign of life, who misinterpret tolerance as indifference toward the question whether or not one's neighbor has found Christ and his Holy Church. We find the spirit of St. Francis and consequently of the true tertiary in the one who observes the words of St. Augustine: *"In necessitatibus unitas; in dubiis libertas; in omnibus caritas."*

The Franciscan spirit, filled with the love of concrete individual beings, respecting the individuality of the creatures of God, seeing a great value in multiplicity, will help the tertiary to see the horror of uniformity in the sphere of culture, economic, and social life. He will see the danger in our present world of destroying all the individual charms of different nations, their cultures, and their way of life, and he will oppose it. In this sphere, in contradistinction to the sphere of religion, pluralism is really a sign of life and a God-given reality of high value.

The true tertiary does not worship illusions of the world as an earthly paradise, nor any sort of terrestrian Messianism. He knows that in our earthly existence, the Cross will remain an inevitable reality. He will not minimize the dangers of this world, nor worship a peaceful coexistence with those who have but one aim: to enslave the whole world, and to destroy the Church. The true tertiary who sees everything in the light of Christ is realistic and abstains from illusions, from an "ostrich policy." But the true tertiary will not despair, because he believes in the words of Christ: *"Et portae inferi non praevalebunt."*

As we saw before, we live in a time characterized by the tendency to claim a right to every good, instead of seeing it as a gift of God, to which we should respond with gratitude. The modern man shuns gratitude; it is vanishing more and more, together with reverence. St. Francis teaches us the virtue of gratitude in a unique way.

Yes, a radiant yet soft light surrounds St. Francis, a light that reflects the glory of the Creator, who surrounds us so lavishly with his goodness and love, who lets "the sun shine on the good and the bad, and lets the rain fall on the just and the unjust." It teaches us, who are apt to focus all our attention on the present moment and who are apt to neglect to see things in their proper perspective, to appreciate earthly beauty as a reflection of the eternal beauty, to understand the message of the setting sun and the far-reaching plains, the sunlit fields, the laughing streams, and the solid rocks, it teaches us, who are apt to take things

90

for granted, to be grateful for the great gifts that come to us from the "Father of light"; it invites us, who are warmed by the sun and delighted by the fragrance of the flowers, who are quickened by the morning coolness and refreshed by a drink of water, who see the stars in the heavens in all their glory and brilliance, to be grateful each day to our heavenly Father and to glow with love toward him whom the heavens praise.

But above all the spirit of St. Francis draws us to an inebriation with the love of Jesus and thus to become totally free, even though we be chained in a prison; the world's hold on us has been broken and the streets and market places are changed into the courtyards of the Church; the poor become rich and the rich become poor in spirit; hardness of heart melts away and we are ready for any sacrifice; deep contrition for our sins will fill our soul, and we long to do penance; and yet a holy joy overflows our soul and victoriously vaults all abysses of suffering; we are made to see that all has meaning and value only in Jesus, from Jesus, through Jesus, for Jesus, and with Jesus.

Does not the deep reverence and touching humility of St. Francis shine resplendent as a light which leads out of the aberrations and darkness of our secularized world? May not for many, the Third Order in its true and original meaning be the way to the apostolate of living a life formed by deep reverence, humility, and true charity?

Many ways lead to Rome. It would radically contradict the spirit of St. Francis and of his Third Order to claim that the Third Order alone offers a way for an unconditional following of Christ, or even that its way would be superior to the way of the oblates or of other lay groups striving for perfection in the world. The fact that St. Francis gave his

91

order the name of *Fratres Minores* testifies to his insist-
ence on humility, not only for the individual but for the
order as well. Any claim to possess a monopoly concerning the way leading to perfection would, therefore, be radically opposed to the spirit of St. Francis.

The way to which someone feels himself attracted is a
question of vocation; it depends on an affinity which does
not carry the conviction that this way must be preferable
for all—as little as love for one's spouse implies the conviction that the beloved is objectively superior to all other
persons.

True, one can also follow St. Francis and take him as
one's model and leader without joining the Third Order.
But as a member of the Third Order one becomes a son
or daughter of St. Francis, a member of a supernatural
family that has existed over seven hundred years; becomes
related in a special manner to all the followers of St. Francis: to St. Elizabeth of Hungary, St. Margaret of Cortona,
St. Louis, Blessed Luchesius, and many others; one shares
a treasure of graces and merits and an abundance of
prayers of intercession; one is taken into the arms of him
who when dying blessed his sons with crossed arms, like
Jacob, and whose sublime prayer reveals so admirably the
way of following Christ:

> Lord, make me an instrument of your peace:
> where there is hatred, let me sow love;
> where there is injury, pardon;
> where there is doubt, faith;
> where there is despair, hope;
> where there is darkness, light;
> and where there is sadness, joy.

O Divine Master, grant that I may not so much seek:
to be consoled as to console,
to be understood as to understand,
to be loved as to love.
For, it is in giving that we receive;
it is in pardoning that we are pardoned;
and it is in dying that we are born to eternal life.